kitchen
essentials

FAY SWEET

kitchen
essentials

RYLAND
PETERS
& SMALL
London New York

Designer Emilie Ekström
Editors Clare Double and Sophie Bevan
Picture research Claire Hector and Emily Westlake
Production Deborah Wehner
Art Director Gabriella Le Grazie
Publishing Director Alison Starling

First published in the United States in 2003
by Ryland Peters & Small, Inc.
519 Broadway
Fifth Floor
New York, NY 10012
www.rylandpeters.com

Library of Congress Cataloging-in-Publication Data

Sweet, Fay.
  Kitchen essentials / Fay Sweet.
    p. cm.
Includes index.
  ISBN 1-84172-482-3
  1. Kitchens. 2. Interior decoration. I. Title.
NK2117.K5 S93 2003
747.7'97--dc21

                                    2003004028

10 9 8 7 6 5 4 3 2 1

Printed and bound in China

contents

getting the elements right

planning the space   8

storage   12

surfaces   18

flooring   22

lighting   25

fixtures   28

putting it together

modern   36

country   42

compact   48

family-friendly   54

resources   60

credits   61

index   64

getting the

elements right

Left The designer has chosen an intriguing place to position this room divider, which incorporates sink, dishwasher, and storage. It straddles a change of levels between rooms linked by a small flight of steps. The long unit encloses the kitchen work area to the left and provides separation from the small lower-level dining area.

Below Open-plan kitchen and living areas give a greater feeling of space, but sometimes you want to be shielded from the sights, sounds, and smells of the kitchen. These sliding panels, suspended from the ceiling, offer a great compromise.

planning the space

If you are designing a new kitchen, or remodeling an old one, start by deciding what type of room would best suit your home and lifestyle. Will it be a family kitchen? Can it be opened up to the living room? Should it be separate from the dining area? Does it need to double as a laundry or home office? And is your kitchen's current site the best location for it—could it be moved to make better use of space, or might it be better accommodated in a new extension?

Left The island and wall units of this elegant kitchen have been given a white finish that harmonizes with the wall color, so the work area takes on a subsidiary role in the room. Only the vast hanging rack offers a visual contrast here.

Below This plan of the same kitchen *(seen left)* shows how the carefully considered design has minimized the impact of the cooking zone on the room as a whole and placed emphasis on the dining area and the window. When you enter this room, your attention is seized by the glass-topped table that stands in front of a large window overlooking the outdoors; meanwhile, the fixtures take second place, sitting neatly along the back wall. A pair of large fridge-freezers have been accommodated in the corner of the room.

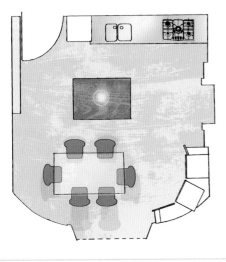

Think about how much and what style of cooking you do. Consider how often you shop, how often you have friends over, whether you like big parties or small intimate dinners. All these things have an impact on the design. If you can cook the way you like with minimal equipment and storage space, don't be tempted to line the room with unnecessary and expensive units. If you shop at the supermarket only once a month, you are likely to need a generous fridge as well as a separate freezer and extra cupboards.

Substantial changes to the layout of the room will affect plumbing and electrical wiring, so take these into account at an early stage. This is also the time to consider whether the lighting plan needs upgrading and to decide if you need new

Opposite above A horseshoe-shaped plan offers division from the dining or living area, while also allowing the cook to keep an eye on children or talk to guests.
Opposite below This kitchen includes a breakfast bar for quick meals as well as a table for more formal dining.
This page Whether you opt for a wall of built-in cabinets, or a more conventional below and above countertop arrangement, plenty of storage space means your surfaces can be kept clear.

appliances, such as a small stove, a big professional-style range, or a dishwasher.

Good kitchen design is revealed in your ease of movement within the "work triangle" of cooktop, fridge, and sink. Avoid siting fridge doors where they would crash into oven doors, and don't place a table in the middle of the busy area between these three elements. Build in plenty of countertop space beside the main fixtures and appliances, so there is room to put down food, hot pans, and plates, as well as for chopping and other preparation.

- **major reorganization** is likely to involve the plumbing, electrical, or gas services

- **lighting upgrades** should be completed before other work

- site appliances for comfort and convenience—**sketch alternative layouts** for the cooktop, fridge, and sink

storage

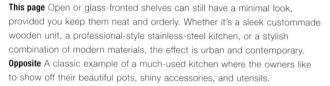

This page Open or glass-fronted shelves can still have a minimal look, provided you keep them neat and orderly. Whether it's a sleek custommade wooden unit, a professional-style stainless-steel kitchen, or a stylish combination of modern materials, the effect is urban and contemporary. **Opposite** A classic example of a much-used kitchen where the owners like to show off their beautiful pots, shiny accessories, and utensils.

There is a universal law about storage: no matter how much you have, you will always need more. So, if you are lucky enough to have room for maneuver, be generous in your estimates. When it comes to deciding on the type of storage you want, most people divide into two camps: those who like to celebrate their possessions by putting them on show, and those who prefer everything hidden neatly out of sight. Knowing which group you belong to will help you choose storage appropriate to your needs.

built-in or not?

Built-in kitchens with their runs of wall and floor units usually offer plenty of storage space, but it is worth comparing them with other forms of storage—the country-style hutch, for example. This single piece of furniture can hold a vast amount of kitchenware and has the advantage of combining closed-in cupboards and open display shelving. If you like open shelving, add a couple of cupboards for unattractive items such as cleaning materials and buckets. Even if you prefer cabinets, I recommend including some open shelving—if only to provide visual relief from the oppression of closed doors.

There are two types of built-in kitchen cabinets: the mass-produced, inexpensive variety that are sold in flat packs; and the up-scale kind that can be tailor-made to your individual design and in the materials of your choice. Although it is unlikely that factory-produced units will be made of the finest woods or built with exquisite

cabinet-making skills, the best of them do an amazing job. They incorporate many useful features, are available in an extensive range of shapes and sizes, and can be individualized by the simple addition of doors and handles of your own choice. On the other hand, if you can afford a taste of genuine luxury, why not hire talented kitchen designers and cabinetmakers to produce works of exceptional beauty and longevity?

Above left Among the excellent features incorporated in these sheer-fronted units is a vertical sliding-drawer pantry.
Above right Back-lit cupboards and shelving not only make it easy to find items, but they also make an intriguing feature—almost like an art work—in the kitchen.
Left Display your dishes to make it quick and easy to find the right plates and cups. Or mix glass- and solid-fronted units for an interesting checkerboard pattern.
Opposite Elements of a traditional style of storage are often borrowed from the professional realm. Any efficient restaurant kitchen will almost certainly include objects such as stainless-steel carts, catering-size metal baking sheets and hanging racks for a whole range of utensils.

People who enjoy the shapes, colors, textures, and simple beauty of kitchen accouterments can find freestanding storage irresistibly appealing. While this style of kitchen exerts a powerful aesthetic appeal, with the additional attractions of comfort and informality, it can also be surprisingly practical. Indeed, the contemporary freestanding look is ideal for anyone who moves house frequently, making it easy to take some of your favorite objects to your new home.

The freestanding kitchen is also particularly appropriate for anyone on a limited budget since, compared with a built-in style, it can be moderately inexpensive to design and put together, and it allows the flexibility to add on when you find another piece of furniture that fits.

details and ergonomics

Since the modern cook is utterly spoiled for choice with the range of utensils, pans, and accessories now on offer, the design of kitchen storage has necessarily been elevated to an exercise in space engineering. Here, attention to detail can make your kitchen a much more satisfying place in which to live and work, and when your kitchen design is complete, you will know that the job has been well done.

In setting out to choose and plan kitchen storage, start by identifying the type of material to be stored. Think about the way you shop and the way you cook. Aim to make sure that items in frequent use are close to you. Think of yourself as the hub of a series of concentric circles. As they radiate out from the center, they represent storage areas for items in different degrees of use. The less something is used, the farther away (or higher up) it can be stored.

The area between waist and shoulder height is the best place for storing most items in frequent use—it is readily accessible and prevents you from having to stretch or bend down too often. Light items should be stored at the top of cabinets, while heavier items are best placed lower down.

Above Ingenious design devices for small spaces include this liftable panel which opens to reveal a toaster.
Right In this well-organized kitchen, the stove is flanked by triple-layer pot stands, which are themselves flanked by drawer units. The stands are handsome items in themselves, comprising slices of dark gray Delabole slate within a stainless-steel frame.
Far right A brilliant piece of design, this chopping board and cart can be wheeled around the kitchen to wherever it is needed. When not in use, it can simply be stowed away in the cupboard.

- **make a list** of the types of item you need to store

- decide if you prefer things **on display or out of sight**

- think about where to **house your most-used items** (baking or pasta-making equipment, for example)

- **auctions and secondhand stores** can be good sources of storage bargains

- an **all-in-one unit** is ideal if you don't cook much or have very little space

- **commission a tailor-made kitchen** only if you have a big budget and are planning to stay in your home for a long time

- **don't overlook details—** build in time to research finishing touches

Above Even in the hardest-working kitchens, there's room for fun. This owner clearly has a sense of humor and has subverted the restrained stainless-steel look with a wild storage rack filled with items in beautiful and colorful packaging.

Far left An unusual but effective style of freestanding storage is to make a frame or shelves into which baskets can be slotted.

Left Kitchen designers are forever coming up with space-saving ideas. A door-fitted rack is an example of how to make the most of difficult corner space.

surfaces

Designed to cope with the endless wear and tear associated with chopping and preparing food, as well as water splashes, countertops and backsplashes are also expected to scrub up beautifully when the cooking is over. In addition, kitchen surfaces can offer an excellent visual and textural opportunity to draw together other stylistic elements of the room's design.

Wood is a perennial favorite for counters. Pale maple or beech can be found in countless kitchens, but darker and more exotically patterned woods are now making an appearance. If you want to incorporate a wooden surface, you need to decide how it will be finished. For example, a beech chopping-board area should be left completely untreated. This tough wood withstands a huge amount of chopping, can cope with fairly hot pans, and scrubs up very well after use.

If you prefer your wood counter to look pristine, a surface finishing is required. Products including Danish oil and tung oil soak into the wood fibers and set hard to repel water and oil splashes, but they need regular maintenance. A tough varnish finish requires minimal maintenance, but cannot be used unprotected for chopping up food or putting down hot pans.

Stainless-steel counters and backsplashes look stunning and, if they are of a high enough grade, will last a lifetime.

Left Making the most of every nook, this custommade laminate counter doubles as a breakfast bar.
Below left A neat hole has been cut into this heavy shelf to fit a small but deep stainless-steel sink.
Below right A flamboyant mixture of colored marbles and stones is pieced together for a work surface and wall finish. Inset is a tiny shelf for ingredients in regular use.
Opposite While tiles are impractical for countertops, they make good backsplashes. Here they continue into the diner-style eating area.

As you use it and clean it, the surface will become covered in a mesh of scratches and marks which develop into a mellow burnish, making stainless steel one of the few counter materials that improves with age and wear.

Another smooth, durable surface that can be welded into long runs and formed into shapes for sinks is a manmade product called Corian. A composite of acrylic resin and natural minerals, it is heat-resistant, stain-resistant, and available in a vast choice of colors. Likewise, plastic laminate surfaces are made in hundreds of colors and patterns, sold by the mile in home-improvement stores. They are tough, easy to clean, and come at a fraction of the cost of most other surfaces.

Natural stone and slate counters have become increasingly sought after in recent years. An enormous slice of shaped marble is a beautiful sight to behold and adds an air of luxury to an elegant kitchen. It is also very

expensive, especially when it includes a hole for a recessed sink and perhaps also tapered grooves for a draining board.

Other stone-type options include stone composites. Several companies are now producing interesting materials by mixing lumps of marble or small speckles of quartzite into a bonding agent such as a resin or a concrete. These are moderately expensive, but do look striking. A further stone-style option is concrete. Forget old-fashioned notions of gray and boring—concrete now comes in all sorts of colors and textures, and can be delivered as a ready-cast countertop or made for you on site.

All types of stone have a porous surface, so ask your supplier what sort of treatment is recommended to avoid staining.

- **wood** makes an excellent work surface; for a perfect finish, seal it with varnish or Danish oil

- **stainless steel** is heatproof and virtually indestructible; a professional grade lasts a lifetime and improves with age and use

- **Corian** is an acrylic and mineral product that can be joined and formed to meet your needs

- **laminate** is tough, good value, and sold in a huge choice of colors and patterns

- **stone and slate** are beautiful, expensive, luxurious, and found in endless variety

- **concrete** can be cast specifically to suit your needs, then polished, finished, and sealed

- **backsplashes** come in a choice of materials, such as stainless steel, stone, glass and plastic glass

Flooring is the major component in any design scheme. It sets the tone of the whole room. In a kitchen it can also devour a big part of your budget, so take care to research well and choose wisely. A canny option is to combine flooring materials—keep warm-toned luxurious wood for the dining area and lay hardworking stone, slate, or linoleum in the cooking area.

Left Small ceramic tiles in black and white produce a stunning geometric pattern that looks particularly handsome alongside the black units, white ceramic sink, and stainless-steel detailing.
Below For a sheer and shimmering mirror finish, specialized high-gloss floor paint has been used on this old wood parquet.
Opposite Bare floorboards wear well and have a pleasing rustic feel.

flooring

Natural materials such as wood, stone, and brick look at home in just about any kitchen. They are hardwearing and durable, but they need protection to keep them looking their best. Wooden flooring is available in finishes ranging from untreated, solid planks to factory-made laminates with a protective vinyl coating. It is important to protect solid, unfinished boards with a varnish, oil, or wax polish. Cork tiles also benefit from a protective coating. Some tiles are sold with a transparent vinyl finish, but if you have chosen a natural tile, it can be sealed with a regular floor varnish.

Other natural materials include hundreds of intriguing stones, marbles, and slates, as well as manmade composites that combine quartz with a resin or cement bonding. Although stone is very hard, it is also porous, so ask your supplier for advice on the most appropriate sealant.

The fashion for wood and stone floors has left sheet and tile finishes rather in the shade. However, there is a huge amount to be said for vinyl, linoleum, and rubber. They are warm, soft, lightweight, relatively easy to lay, fairly forgiving of slightly uneven floors—and the choice is more extensive than ever. On top of that, they look good in just about any style of kitchen; they are considerably cheaper than wood or stone alternatives, require no finishing, and are very easy to keep clean. Also available are big panels of stainless steel or aluminum, which are unusual and eyecatching, and look great held in place with lines of neat rivets.

Below, from left to right Speckled patterns, like this composite made from colored stones, are highly practical in heavily used family kitchens—they don't require constant cleaning. Diamond and square tiles create a lively pattern. Sterlingboard tiles are an inexpensive option and produce this interesting effect. Studded rubber is stylish, modern, and hardwearing.

- the **floor base** should be sound and stable, and strong enough to carry the weight of your chosen material

- **wood** is a sympathetic option, ranging from ready-made interlocking systems to solid boards

- much underrated, **cork** is hardwearing, an efficient sound-absorber, a good looker, and feels warm to the touch

- **stone** is a big investment, but it provides a tough finish that will last a lifetime

- **concrete**—painted, waxed, or varnished—has become a favorite in modern interiors

- **linoleum and vinyl**, stylish and excellent value, are the unsung heroes of the kitchen

Above Sheet metal flooring is a stylish, hardworking option for the kitchen, with a strong industrial aesthetic. However, it can be slippery, and is unforgiving on dropped china.

Right Wood flooring adds a sense of warmth and texture to an all-white room that is otherwise sleek and hard-edged. A solid, machine-made flooring such as cut stone slabs could have made this room feel chilly and uninviting.

lighting

Kitchen lighting must give good, safe illumination for work areas and comfortable ambient lighting for the main part of the room, and be flexible enough to cope with a variety of dining situations. To achieve the range of effects you desire, you will probably need to incorporate a variety of lighting types.

Above Lighting should be attractive as well as practical. Here shelf-mounted downlighters illuminate the work surface and the wall-mounted lamp on an extending arm can be positioned to wherever it is required.
Right The choice of lighting types for kitchens is vast: from suspended pendant lights with brushed-aluminum or glass shades, to these unusual office-style lamps on jointed arms and tiny sparkling fixtures that can be built into the underside of units. The best lighting plans will incorporate a number of different styles to achieve results that are both practical and aesthetic.

Far left This under-cupboard light illuminates the work surface, while its integrated baffle reduces glare.
Left A string of theatrical twinkling bulbs around a window enhances the atmosphere of the space.
Below The ethereal quality of this space—with its white cabinets and linen shade—is picked up and continued in the use of artificial lighting.
Opposite A handsome pair of large pendant lights provides general, ambient lighting, while the wall-mounted spots shed light on the work surface and sink.

When you start to plan a scheme, take stock of the lighting that is already in existence. Make notes about where it falls short, which lights need to be moved or added, and what style of lighting you would like to install. This is also the moment to have your wiring checked and to decide whether it would be helpful to have more electrical sockets.

The importance of good functional lighting, or task lighting, cannot be overestimated. The kitchen is full of potential hazards—sharp knives, hot water, and heavy pans, to name but a few—and it is the site of more accidents than any other room in the home. Task lighting should provide counters with high levels of illumination and be positioned so that you are not standing in your own shadow. It is a good idea to install these functional lights on a separate circuit from the main room lights, so that they can be dimmed or turned off completely when they are not needed.

In addition to task lighting, the room will require a general wash of ambient illumination that helps to shape the overall space. This is usually provided by a central pendant, wall lights, or a ceiling-mounted track that can be angled to direct light across the ceiling or down the walls.

Sparkling-white halogen lights are a popular choice for use in track systems or to highlight particular features of a room. Fluorescent tubes are most frequently employed for countertop lighting, attached to the bottom of wall cabinets. An alternative to the fluorescent tube is the tungsten tube, which gives out a lovely, soft, creamy-colored light. Then there is the trusty tungsten lightbulb—useful in pendant lights suspended over tables and for large spotlights.

• **list the advantages and disadvantages** of your current scheme and decide on the priorities for improvement

• **call in an engineer** to check the safety of your entire electrical wiring system

• **install plenty of task lights**—to avoid shadows, they should be just above and in front of someone standing at the counter, cooktop, or sink

• take the opportunity to **add electrical sockets** if they are needed

• **fixtures should be both beautiful and practical:** have fun with ambient lighting to enhance the aesthetic appeal of your home

• **add unusual details** such as useful lights inside cupboards —glass-fronted cabinets look stunning lit from inside

fixtures

Choosing fixtures and appliances can be exciting, confusing, and expensive. It is easy to be drawn toward minimal designs or sophisticated models that promise to run the kitchen for you, but think carefully about what you cook and how you cook it, and base your selection on what seems most appropriate to your needs. As always, practicality should be high on your list of priorities.

Above Incorporating a countertop, a two-burner cooktop, and an inset circular sink and faucet, this sweep of stainless steel makes impressively good use of a confined space.
Left This capacious fridge and freezer unit is ideal for a large family kitchen where lots of food needs to be stored in a cool place. The doors are finished in the same sleek metal as the rest of the kitchen, which helps reduce the visual bulk of the appliance.

sinks and faucets

The wet area of the kitchen demands as much design thought as elsewhere. You will probably use the sink every time you prepare food, so your choice should be based on practical requirements. If you have ever had to wash roasting pans in a tiny circular sink, you will know how frustrating it can be.

For something simple and exceptionally good value, a standard pressed-steel sink unit is hard to beat. Among the other delights on offer are sinks of every shape in beaten copper, glass, enamel, acrylic, and the handsome and trusty Belfast sink in white ceramic. In recent years there has been a move away from built-in draining boards. Be warned: a sink without a draining board may look wonderfully sleek and

minimal, but once those roasting pans have been washed, you will want to leave them to drain before putting them away.

There is a huge variety of faucets available, from old-fashioned cross-heads to modern mixers with a multitude of additional features. Since faucets are probably the most frequently used fixture in a kitchen, it is worth investing in the best possible quality.

Left, above and below Generously sized sinks and large draining areas necessarily take up space, but are very welcome in kitchens where lots of different styles of cooking take place, using large trays, saucepans, or awkwardly shaped items like woks.
Above right A reinvention of the Belfast sink: here a wooden "chest" sink sits inside a specially made curved concrete cradle.
Right Two sinks are always better than one—this arrangement leaves one for washing, one for rinsing.

- **the sink's size and shape** should reflect your style of cooking—if you cook roasts, for example, it must be large enough to take a roasting pan

- **draining boards** are more useful than you might think: if space is tight, a small draining area is better than none

- **faucets** can incorporate a multitude of added features, but think hard about whether you really need the extras

- **water softeners** installed in hard-water areas prevent the build-up of mineral deposits and consequent damage to stainless-steel sinks and faucets

Above Good-quality cross-head faucets are a wise investment, but don't take things too seriously—cheer the place up with varnished 1950s postcards.
Left Faucets are now excitingly multifunctional. It is still possible to buy reliable old-fashioned sets with cross-head tops, but many designs feature pull-out ends and flexible spouts for washing fruit and vegetables.

fridges and freezers

Long regarded as boring white boxes, fridge-freezers have at last gained recognition as great design objects, and models are appearing in a range of shapes, sizes, and colors to suit people's tastes and their shopping habits.

An integrated fridge is an expensive item, but it does have the advantage that it sits behind a cupboard door without taking up a vast amount of space. Other options include choosing big boxy fridges and then having a frame made to disguise its bulk. Among the most attractive innovations are fridges with glass fronts, which mimic those in professional kitchens and food stores. These are sleek pieces of design, often made with glass set inside a stainless-steel frame.

Most of us are happy to make do with a half or third of the fridge devoted to shelves or pull-out trays for frozen goods. If you need more capacity, there are upright or chest freezers in a whole range of sizes, but these have remained untouched by developments in contemporary design.

Above Fridges needn't be hidden behind cabinet doors. If you have chosen a stunning fridge, it will stand happily on show and look great. The old '50s refrigerator—whose characterful, rounded shape made it much sought after in its day—is enjoying a popular revival. Likewise, modern brightly colored models are particularly attractive.

Left As the fridge has taken over from the pantry, many families are opting for capacious double refrigerators, or buying a pair of fridges or a fridge and freezer to stand side by side.

Near right State-of-the-art cooktops are dramatically increasing the responsiveness of electric appliances.

Center right Tiny electric burners are ideal for tasks like making the best espresso coffee or warming soup. They are very efficient and great space-savers in a small kitchen—ideal for anyone who does little cooking.

Far right The old-fashioned range is more than just a stove: it is the hub of the kitchen where people love to warm themselves against the toasty hot doors. They can sometimes double as tanks to supply the home with hot water and central heating.

Below A vast stainless-steel cooktop with different types of gas burners and two close-down covers is the main feature of this exciting set-up.

Opposite, main If you don't like all your appliances on show, stow away the microwave when not in use.

ovens and cooktops

When it comes to identifying the perfect cooking arrangement, people usually fall into two camps: those who like a built-in oven with a separate cooktop and those who prefer a freestanding stove. As a broad general rule, the built-in oven appeals most to those people who like order, fingertip control, and the latest technology. By contrast, freestanding stoves have a more diverse fan club.

For a start, there are two main types of freestanding stoves. At one end of the spectrum is the regular slide-in machine. At the other is the great big, semi-professional stove or range. The principal differences between the two concern size and price. While the humble machine is comparable in price to a weekend break, the range will cost the equivalent of a small car.

- **freestanding or built-in?** Start by identifying your preferred style of oven

- **country or professional?** If you choose to have a freestanding model, decide which style is best suited to the design and layout of your room

- **gas or electric?** Many cooks feel the best combination is a gas cooktop and electric oven. The fuel available in your area will have an important bearing on your choice

- **state-of-the-art or straightforward?** If you can't understand the controls in the showroom, it probably means hours of poring over the manual

Deciding to install a built-in stove and cooktop in separate locations will give you much more flexibility in the layout of your kitchen. The oven can be located almost anywhere under the countertop or at waist level in a wall-mounted unit. Cooktops can then be positioned in one of any number of places on the countertop.

Base your final choice of oven and burners on your style of cooking. If you are an infrequent cook, are you prepared to spend a small fortune on appliances that will remain largely unused? If you are a regular cook, do you have the budget to invest in the equipment of your dreams?

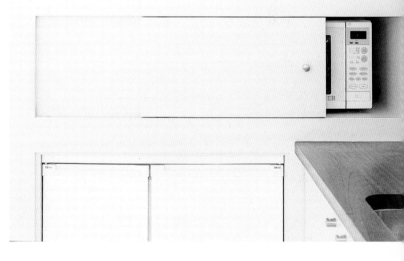

putting it

together

modern

Ultra-modern kitchens are essays in exquisite finishes and expert craftsmanship. They are rigorously designed and highly industrialized products with controlled, crisp edges, which seem absolutely appropriate in big, stripped-back, minimally furnished apartments, converted warehouses, and former factory buildings. However, while such a style of kitchen is frequently associated with loft apartments, it can look just as good in old barns and farmhouses.

Far left The loft apartment is the natural home for a contemporary-style kitchen. The factory-made stainless-steel units complement the tough, urban warehouse aesthetic with its metal windows and smooth plastered walls.

Left and below This stainless-steel design is based on the professional kitchens found in hotels and restaurants, but luxuries like a marble backsplash would never be found in a commercial kitchen.

The key features of the sleek and contemporary style are runs of built-in floor and wall cupboards. These might be painted or lacquered, or made to incorporate a metal-mesh or glass-paneled front. Work surfaces are often made of stone, concrete, stainless steel, or a manmade material such as a quartz composite or Corian. Appliances are ultra-modern and probably built in. Lighting features low-voltage halogen bulbs to provide a sparkling clean white light. Where there is room for a dining table within the kitchen, it is almost certain to be contemporary in style, too.

Within the overall style, there is plenty of room for experimentation. People who want a more professional-looking finish will opt for durable and crisp hard surfaces: stainless steel for units, countertops, and appliance doors; stone for flooring; glass for door fronts or shelves; and white or neutral-colored walls. These elements will be complemented by plain and elegant accessories: contemporary-style chrome faucets,

Above True to the modern look, every feature and surface in this kitchen has been carefully considered and beautifully finished. The mid-tone wood appears on the monumental room-divider unit and then again on the smaller wall units opposite. The palette is completed with the use of opaque glass on cupboard fronts and a shiny black table top.

Left The state-of-the-art oven and sleek finishes leave no doubt that this is the kitchen of someone who appreciates high-quality modern design. The table and bench, in a darker wood than the cabinets, share the same aesthetic.

Left An exquisite example of fine engineering: beautiful stainless-steel doors are topped by a continuous stainless-steel work surface and built-in sink. On the wall, slender open shelves show off white china, stainless steel, and glassware.

Right top Wood is used in a restrained and modern way in these mesh-fronted cupboards.

Right center Although designed half a century ago, these Series 7 chairs by Arne Jacobsen still look contemporary and help to create an interior that is both modern and timeless.

Right bottom The coolness of stainless steel, white laminate, and plexiglass is offset by the use of warm walnut tones for these kitchen cabinets.

industrial-style electrical sockets and light switches, professional pans and utensils, and simple white china.

Mixing metal and wood is another way to interpret the contemporary style. The ideal setting for a "mixed" kitchen is a space that is well illuminated with natural sunlight and which has beautifully finished floors and plain painted or tiled walls. The industrial toughness of metal can be offset by wood finishes. Stainless steel and chrome look great with a whole range of wood tones, from honey-colored cherry and maple to the richest, darkest wenge. Open-grained softwoods such as pine do not combine well with metal, but stainless steel does have a strong affinity with plywood. The key to success is to restrict the combination of metal and wood to just two different materials, and certainly no more than three. Try stainless-steel countertops with metal-and-maple cupboard doors and then maple again for the floor. Explore the up-scale contemporary-style kitchen showrooms to see how this works best. Finishing touches are crucial, too: beautiful carpentry, long metal handles or push-release mechanisms for doors, and lighting that makes the place sparkle.

modular units—in **painted, lacquered, tough laminate, or sheet-steel finishes**—are the building blocks of the style

order and organization are key, with **closed storage space and surfaces kept clear** of equipment and accessories

streamlined modern elements ...

lighting features **crisp halogen** lamps, but build in softer options such as **aluminum or glass pendants**

furniture has metal frames; tables are topped with **glass, laminate, stone, or highly polished wood**

invest in high-quality fixtures and workmanship

from the professional kitchen

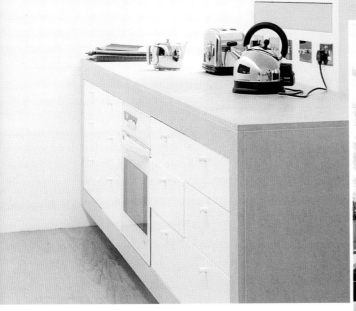

country

The style has its roots in the traditional farmhouse kitchen—which could be virtually anywhere in the Western world. Ideas and details are drawn from places as far apart as Tuscany and Devon, Philadelphia and Provence. While this kitchen is a comfortable nest of nostalgia, it remains a highly functional workplace that has stood the test of time. Big cast-iron stoves and ranges are ideal for family cooking, hutches have enormous storage capacity, highly durable floors withstand most of what is thrown at them, and farmhouse tables are rugged and virtually indestructible.

Left The generously sized room and use of wood for cabinets and flooring combine to make this a truly robust workplace. From the rack of pans to the pots of utensils and the big stove, this is clearly a place for serious cooking. A nice touch is added by the hanging baskets of fruit and vegetables—just unhook and refill them out in the garden.

Right The country look is unmistakable, with the big ceramic sink, racks of pots hung to dry, wood-finished walls, and herbs sitting on the sunny window ledge.

Below, left and right There's a certain jolly chaos to the country look, a sense of abundance and generosity. This is a place to linger. In contrast to its urban cousin, the country kitchen is a place for pattern. Whether your style is country cottage rosebuds or retro prints, fabrics are a must in completing the look.

Although today's country kitchen bears a strong resemblance to its predecessors, under the scrubbed-down surfaces lurk the dishwashers, fridge-freezers, and lighting systems of modern life. After establishing the traditional character of the space by installing an enamel stove or range, some form of natural flooring, and appropriate furniture, it becomes possible gradually to mix in a few modern items—perhaps a run of built-in cupboards or a track of spotlights.

The skill in creating a successful mixture of old and new is to make sure the interventions are sensitive to the overall look. Anything that is too highly finished will jar with the mellowness of the room. The same thinking should be applied to details such as tiling and faucets, shelving and furniture—items should all maintain an air of simplicity.

A visit to an architectural salvage yard could yield some real finds in the shape of period sinks, tiles, or furniture. Take care when buying secondhand goods—some older items such

Above The country style is flagged up here in no uncertain terms: the jolly checked fabric of the sofa takes front of stage while behind, the small kitchen features lots of open shelves for showing off intriguing objects. The wood floor completes the look.

Right This restrained country look is carefully orchestrated right from the display of white enamel saucepans on top of the plate rack to the built-in hutch with its blue and white china. This room has a limited palette of white and wood, with interest added in the blue of the china, the wicker basket, and the garlic hanging by the stove.

Far left The white theme with accents of red is a real breath of fresh air. This is clearly a rural kitchen, but it has an interesting modern edge.
Left Here is a version of a rural retro style—the blue and white theme has a strong '50s feel, and the painted cupboard combines simplicity with practicality.
Below An example of the Shaker style of kitchen which works so well in town and country. The cream-colored cabinets are elegantly designed with just a little detail in the arch shape of the doors.

as faucets might no longer be compatible with modern plumbing. There are also plenty of stores selling new kitchen products in retro styles: enameled freestanding fridges, '50s-style food mixers, Formica-topped tables and chairs, and a vast array of period lamps.

Among the most popular versions of the style in recent years have been the Shaker-style kitchen and kitchens with a lighter, Scandinavian look. In both cases, many classic country elements survive: natural flooring materials, wood-built units and countertops, and deep ceramic sinks. Yet today's version is more sophisticated, more efficient even, than the original.

The country-style kitchen sits just as happily in an urban setting—a testament to the versatility of the traditional style. Its look is less important than its ambience, which is informal, comfortable, and welcoming.

an easy-to-live-with style ...

you needn't spend a fortune to achieve this homey, welcoming look

flagstones, large terracotta tiles, or wooden floorboards set the scene

countertops are **pale maple**, or for a sophisticated alternative choose **slate or marble**

research your period look—visit museums, read books—and keep an eye out for the furnishings and all-important details that reflect the style

accessories—build up a collection of antique kitchen utensils, such as butter molds, milk jugs, stone water bottles

in natural materials

compact

Although there is no room for waste or error when you are planning the layout of a small kitchen, there is plenty of space for big ideas to make even the tiniest area work efficiently. A small galley might at first glance look like the toughest design challenge, but in many ways the smaller the kitchen, the easier the job. There is an abundance of examples to follow: tiny kitchens on barges and boats, all-in-one studio kitchens, and the small cupboard-sized efficiencies that can be found in many offices.

Opposite In addition to providing storage space, the custom-made wall cupboards disguise an extractor vent. Fitted to the underside of the cupboards is the base of the extractor; the action of pulling it forward switches on the fan and in-built lights. The rest of the unit is housed inside the cupboards.

Left This horseshoe-shaped arrangement, with stove at one end, makes an efficient work space for one person, with just about everything within arm's reach.

Below Built-in cupboards mean that no space is wasted and make it possible to stow everything away, right down to the cookbooks. With clutter out of sight, the kitchen is kept in an orderly fashion.

Left Small kitchens like this are a triumph of space engineering. It is an incredibly satisfying piece of design, combining all the basics of sink, cooktop, microwave, and fridge, and featuring an unusual upper tier of cupboards at ceiling level for items least often in use.
Below A good idea in small kitchens is to have open shelves above the work surface. In a confined space—particularly a narrow galley—shelves tend to be less oppressive that a row of closed cupboards.

Be optimistic. Small can be beautiful. With a little invention it is entirely possible to create delicious, full-scale meals on just a double burner. The first step is to take a look at the space available and make realistic plans. Spend as much time as possible planning your layout—time spent working on paper will save frustrations later on. What sort of cooking do you want to carry out in your kitchen? What style of kitchen do you prefer? The sleek modern look is probably the most space-efficient, but there's nothing to stop you from making a friendly country-style space.

Start with the basics: a sink, fridge, cooktop, and oven. In each case it is now possible to buy scaled-down versions. It's even possible to find countertop dishwashers and washing machines. With the appliances in mind, assess how much storage may be required. Here's the key to a successful compact kitchen—use every available nook. The cleverest kitchens incorporate all sorts of great ideas, including large drawers at floor level in place of plinths, swing-out corner carousels, cupboards that stretch to the ceiling, fold-down tables, and so on. Also consider whether a cupboard can be located elsewhere in the home. For example, a hutch in the dining room could house china and flatware, freeing up a kitchen cupboard to locate the washing machine.

Try to maximize the natural light available in the room, and make sure you have really good artificial lighting. A compact kitchen is certainly a challenge, but when designed with great care, it is also a real pleasure to cook in.

reduced to bare essentials ...

be realistic in your aims and **resist crowding** the space—dispense with items you rarely use

opt for scaled-down appliances and use every available nook and cranny

make the most of new and **innovative design ideas,** such as big drawers at floor level instead of plinths

sheer, shining surfaces in pale colors reflect light, giving a sense of space

built-in cupboards provide maximum storage space

relocate items, such as the washing machine, to elsewhere in the home

keep windows unobstructed and install **high levels of artificial lighting**

the compact kitchen triumphs

family-friendly

With the kitchen as the hub of the home, it is a place for family and friends to congregate. The style should be relaxed, flexible, and welcoming as well as safe, hygienic, and highly durable. Don't be afraid to add a splash of color and interesting details like blackboards, toy cupboards, and a play corner. An open-plan design is perfect for families, enabling adults to cook while also keeping a watchful eye over children playing, eating, or doing their homework.

Far left Two large fridge-freezers are sited in the corner of this kitchen behind blackboard-covered doors. Parents can use the upper part of the blackboards for writing messages, while children use the lower portion.

Left Open-plan living can be ideal for growing families. While parents are cooking, they can keep an eye on children at play. This home incorporates a small family dining area close to the kitchen, ideal for children, as well as a larger dining area further into the space, for more formal entertaining.

Below Irresistible child-friendly details like these chair backs make mealtimes more enjoyable.

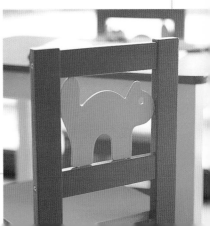

The key to getting a family-friendly kitchen right is to create a space where children and adults can spend time together and separately, getting on with their tasks without getting under each other's feet. Having adequate space to accommodate everyone is vital, so very small kitchens are far from ideal, unless there is the opportunity to link them with an adjoining living or dining area.

The style of kitchen can be modern or country, but uppermost in your mind must be making sure that children can play in safety while adults cook. When planning the space, a good solution for harmonious relations is to make a designated area for children—include a child-size table and chairs, a soft play area, a toy box, space for books and games, a television, or computer.

In designing the kitchen, make sure it is possible to keep an eye on children while also keeping dangerous and heavy kitchen items well out of reach. It may be necessary to include locked cupboards. Remember also that children love to help in the kitchen, so perhaps add a chair or steps so they can reach the work surface to roll pastry or play in the sink.

All surfaces need to be tough and wipe-clean washable. Floors must be easy to mop or brush: linoleum, vinyl, wood with a tough varnish finish, sealed stone, and ceramic are all good. The same goes for units: doors with lots of detail and ledges will collect dust and food, so sheer finishes are preferable. Incorporate rounded corners where possible, particularly at child's eye level.

Children love colorful environments, so be as wild as you like with the scheme. For a restrained effect, paint just one or two walls in bright colors, or add color in the form of accessories or furniture. As ever, good electric lighting is a must, and will allow you to switch from bright lights at children's snack time to a subtle effect for entertaining.

Opposite A dining room-kitchen arrangement is ideal for families with children. A robust kitchen table doubles as a desk for homework, while long benches allow everyone to squeeze in at mealtimes.

Above The use of bold colors and attention to detail make family-friendly kitchens fun. The witty upside-down teacup shade can't fail to raise a smile; robust old chairs and fruit boxes are painted different colors for a new lease on life; and pots and pans are festooned with jolly garlands.

Left Children automatically mean greater wear and tear on the home, so durable finishes such as extra-tough varnish used on wood floors and cupboards are essential for keeping the place looking smart.

make a **play area** for children with a toy box, books, and child-sized table and chairs

incorporate a chair or steps that reach up to the work surface so **little hands can learn and help** with the cooking

add a splash of **color and fun** details like blackboards

thoughtful design ...

durable, wipe-clean surfaces
are a must, such as wood
flooring with a tough varnish
finish, linoleum, or vinyl

safety is key: design out any
sharp corners, and keep
sharp, heavy, and hot objects
out of harm's way

flexible lighting can switch
from a kid's supper to an
adult dinner party

with space and interest for everyone

resources

ABC Carpet & Home
212 473 3000
www.abchome.com
Furnishings and lighting.

AGA Ranges
800 633 9200
Traditional cookers.

American Floor Products
800 342 0424
Rubber and vinyl tile flooring.

The Antique Hardware and Home Store
800 422 9982
www.antiquehardware.com
Reproduction sinks and faucets.

Blanco
800 451 5782
www.blanco-america.com
Sinks and accessories.

Broan
800 558 1711
www.broan.com
Ventilation hoods in enamel colors and stainless steel.

Bruck Lighting Systems
714 424 0500
www.brucklighting.com
Track and cable lighting.

Bulthaup
800 808 2923
www.bulthaup.com
Contemporary kitchen design.

Colonial Craft Kitchens
717 867 1145
www.colonialkitchens.com
Custom-made cabinets.

Crate & Barrel
800 996 9960
www.crateandbarrel.com
Good-value furniture and accessories.

Dakota Granite
www.dakgran.com
Granite counters and floors.

Designs Of The Century
212 410 1200
Kitchen cabinetry, surfaces, and accessories.

DuPont Corian
800 426 7426
www.dupont.com/corian
Acrylic surface used for sinks and countertops.

Fishs Eddy
889 Broadway
New York, NY 10011
212 420 2090
'50s-style china.

Formica
800 638 4380
www.formica.com
Laminate surfaces.

Franke
800 626 5771
www.frankeksd.com
High-quality sink systems, faucets, and accessories.

Hafele America Company
800 334 1873
www.hafeleonline.com
Recessed lights.

Hansgrohe
800 719 1000
www.hansgrohe.com
High-quality, European-designed faucets.

HomeClick.com
800 643 9990
www.homeclick.com
Luxury sinks, faucets, cabinets, and accessories.

Ikea
Mail order and online store:
www.ikea.com
Home basics at great prices, including furniture and stylish, inexpensive kitchenware.

Juno Lighting
800 323 5068
www.junolighting.com
Sleek, modern track and recessed lighting.

Kahrs International
800 800 5247
www.kahrs.com
Wood floors to suit high-traffic areas, such as kitchens.

Kohler
800 456 4537
www.kohlerco.com
Sinks in enamels and metals, faucets, and accessories.

KraftMaid Cabinetry
888 562 7744
www.kraftmaid.com
Cabinetry in traditional and contemporary styles.

Moen
800 553 6636
www.moen.com
Good-quality faucets.

National Kitchen and Bath Association.
For information on members in your area, call 800 401 NKBA or 800 367 6522.

Northland
800 223 3900
www.northlandnka.com
Customized refrigerators and freezers in virtually any size.

Poggenpohl
800 987 0553
www.poggenpohl-usa.com
European kitchen design.

Pottery Barn
800 922 5507
www.potterybarn.com
Furniture and accessories.

Price Pfister
800 732 8238
www.pricepfister.com
Elegant kitchen faucets.

Rapetti Faucets
800 688 5500
High-end faucets at reasonable prices.

Restoration Hardware
800 816 0901
www.restorationhardware.com
Furniture, lighting, and accessories.

Sears, Roebuck
800 MY-SEARS
www.sears.com
Resurfacing of cabinets and drawers for a new look.

Sheldon Slate
207 997 3615
www.sheldonslate.com

Sub-Zero
800 222 7820
www.subzero.com
Custom-made refrigerators.

Urban Outfitters
628 Broadway
New York, NY 10012
212 475 0009
www.urbanoutfitters.com
Trendy tableware and accessories.

Val Cucine
866 468 2636
Ultra-cool, professional-style kitchens.

Viking Designer Kitchens
888 845 4641
www.vikingrange.com
Professional-style kitchens.

Wellborn Cabinet
800 336 8040 ext. 216
www.wellborncabinet.com
Wooden cabinets for a custom-designed look.

Williams-Sonoma
800 541 1262
www.williams-sonomainc.com
Cooking utensils, fine linens, and classic china.

credits

Key: a=above, b=below, r=right, l=left, c=center, ph = photographer

Endpapers ph Jan Baldwin/Jan Hashey and Yasuo Minagawa; **1** ph Catherine Gratwicke/Lulu Guinness's home in London; **2** ph Andrew Wood/Phillip Low, New York; **3** ph Polly Wreford/home of 27.12 Design Ltd., Chelsea, NYC; **4l** ph Andrew Wood; **4c** ph Polly Wreford/Clare Nash's house in London; **4r** ph Polly Wreford; **5** ph Polly Wreford/The Sawmills Studios; **6–7** ph Chris Everard/Nadav Kander & Nicole Verity's house; **8l** ph James Merrell/a house in Sydney designed by Luigi Rosselli; **8r** ph Andrew Wood/Nik Randall, Suzsi Corio and Louis' home in London designed by Brookes Stacey Randall; **9** ph Chris Everard/Kampfner's house in London designed by Ash Sakula Architects; **9** illustration by Shonagh Rae; **10a** ph Andrew Wood/Nello Renault's loft in Paris; **10b** ph Chris Everard/Hudson Street Loft, designed by Moneo Brock Studio; **11l** ph Andrew Wood/Andrew Noble's apartment in London designed by Nico Rensch Architeam; **11r** ph Chris Everard/designed by Mullman Seidman Architects; **12l** ph Andrew Wood/a house in London designed by Bowles and Linares; **12c** ph Chris Everard/Vicson Guevara's apartment in New York designed by Yves-Claude Design; **12r** ph Chris Everard/David Mullman's apartment in New York designed by Mullman Seidman Architects; **13** ph Chris Everard/the London apartment of the Sheppard Day Design Partnership; **14al** ph Chris Everard/Hudson Street Loft, designed by Moneo Brock Studio; **14ar** ph James Merrell/a house in Pennsylvania designed by Laura Bohn and built by Richard Fiore/BFI Construction; **14bl** ph Alan Williams/Margot Feldman's house in New York designed by Patricia Seidman of Mullman Seidman Architects; **14br** ph Alan Williams/Katie Bassford King's house in London designed by Touch Interior Design; **15l** ph Alan Williams/interior designer and Managing Director of the Société Yves Halard, Michelle Halard's own apartment in Paris; **15r** ph Andrew Wood/Alastair Hendy & John Clinch's apartment in London designed by Alastair Hendy; **16a** ph Chris Everard/Hudson Street Loft, designed by Moneo Brock Studio; **16bl** ph Andrew Wood/Ian Bartlett & Christine Walsh's house in London; **16br** ph Chris Everard/Vicson Guevara's apartment in New York designed by Yves-Claude Design; **17a** ph Catherine Gratwicke/Kimberley Watson's house in London; **17bl** ph Andrew Wood/Dawna & Jerry Walter's house in London; **17br** ph Chris Everard/florist and landscape designer Stephen Woodhams' home in London, designed by architect Taylor Hammond, kitchen by Camarque; **18** ph Jan Baldwin/Emma Wilson's house in London; **19l** ph Chris Everard/an apartment in New York designed by Gabellini Associates; **19ar** ph Chris Everard/Michael Nathenson's house in London; **19br** ph Jan Baldwin/Constanze von Unruh's house in London; **20a** ph Chris Everard/designed by Filer & Cox, London; **20bl** ph Andrew Wood/Alastair Hendy & John Clinch's apartment in London designed by Alastair Hendy; **20br** ph James Merrell/Consuelo Zoelly's apartment in Paris; **21** ph Chris Everard/an apartment in New York designed by Steven Learner; **22l** ph Chris Everard/a house in London designed by Helen Ellery of The Plot London; **22r** ph Alan Williams/the architect Voon Wong's own apartment in London; **23a** ph Jan Baldwin/Emma Wilson's house in London; **23bl** ph Chris Everard/Gentucca Bini's apartment in Milan; **23bcl** ph James Merrell/a house in Sydney designed by Luigi Rosselli; **23bcr** ph Chris Everard/Ian Chee of VX design & architecture; **23br** ph Chris Everard/Andrew Wilson's apartment in London designed by Azman Owens; **24l** ph Henry Bourne/DAD Associates; **24r** ph Henry Bourne/a house in London designed by Mark Guard Architects; **25a** ph Ray Main/a house in London designed by Ash Sakula Architects; **25cl** ph James Merrell/an apartment in London designed by Ash Sakula Architects; **25bl** ph Ray Main/light from Hector Finch; **25bc** ph Andrew Wood/Alastair Hendy & John Clinch's apartment in London designed by Alastair Hendy; **25br** ph Ray Main/Jonathan Reed's apartment in London, lighting designed by Sally Storey, Design Director of John Cullen Lighting; **26l** ph Ray Main/a loft in London designed by Circus Architects, light from Fulham Kitchens; **26c** ph James Merrell/Stephen Woodhams' house in London designed in conjunction with Mark Brook Design; **26r** ph Ray Main/a house in London designed by Seth Stein and Sarah Delaney; **27** ph Ray Main; **28l** ph Chris Everard/John Barman's Park Avenue apartment; **28r** ph Andrew Wood/Andrew Noble's apartment in London designed by Nico Rensch Architeam; **29al** ph Henry Bourne; **29bl** ph Andrew Wood/Phillip Low, New York; **29ar** ph Jan Baldwin/Emma Wilson's house in London; **29br** ph James Merrell/Andrew Arnott and Karin Schack's house in Melbourne; **30a** ph Catherine Gratwicke/Martin Barrell & Amanda Sellers' flat, owners of Maisonette, London; **30bl** ph Christopher Drake/Melanie Thornton's house in Gloucestershire; **30bc** ph James Merrell/Felix Bonnier's apartment in Paris; **30br** ph Chris Everard/François Muracciole's apartment in Paris; **31b** ph James Merrell/Douglas and Dorothy Hamilton's apartment in New York; **31al** ph Chris Everard/Gentucca Bini's apartment in Milan; **31ar** ph Andrew Wood; **32l** ph James Merrell/Felix Bonnier's apartment in Paris; **32r** ph Chris Everard/Arlene Hirst's New York kitchen designed by Steven Sclaroff; **32–33** ph Chris Everard/designed by Filer & Cox, London; **33l** ph Jan Baldwin/Constanze von Unruh's house in London; **33r** ph Chris Everard/photographer Guy Hills' house in London designed by Joanna Rippon and Maria Speake of Retrouvius; **34–35** ph Andrew Wood/Rosa Dean & Ed Baden-Powell's apartment in London, designed by Urban Salon; **36** ph Jan Baldwin/David Gill's house in London; **36–37** ph Chris Everard/Vicson Guevara's apartment in New York designed by Yves-Claude Design; **38l** ph Chris Everard/an actor's London home designed by Site Specific; **38r** ph Ray Main/Kenneth Hirst's apartment in New York; **39l** ph Jan Baldwin/Christopher Leach's apartment in London; **39ar** ph Henry Bourne/Felix Bonnier's apartment in Paris; **39cr** ph Andrew Wood/Chelsea loft apartment in New York, designed by The Moderns; **39br** ph Chris Everard/architect Jonathan Clark's home in London; **40a** ph Alan Williams/the architect Voon Wong's own apartment in London; **40bl** ph Andrew Wood/Gabriele Sanders' apartment in New York, chairs from Totem; **40br** ph Chris Everard/Ou Baholyodhin & Erez Yardeni's penthouse, Highpoint, London; **41l** ph Andrew Wood/Robert Kimsey's apartment in London designed by Gavin Jackson; **41ar** ph Chris Everard/Ian Chee of VX design & architecture; **41br** ph Debi Treloar/new build house in Notting Hill designed by Seth Stein Architects; **42–43** ph Alan Williams/Andrew Wallace's house in London; **43ar** ph Chris Everard/a house in London designed by Helen Ellery of The Plot London; **43bl** ph Catherine Gratwicke/Lucy and Marc Salem's London home, free-standing "retro" kitchen by Marc & Lucy Salem; **43br** ph Catherine Gratwicke/Rose Hammick's home in London. French enamelled tins from Grace & Favour, 1950s curtains from Alexandra Fairweather; **44a** ph Catherine Gratwicke/Rose Hammick's home in London. Checked sofa cover & red toile cushion from Nicole Fabre, 1920s gold cushion from Kim Sully Antiques; **44b** ph Henry Bourne; **45l&c** ph Chris Tubbs/Mike and Deborah Geary's beach house in Dorset; **45r** ph Simon Upton; **46al** ph Tom Leighton; **46bl** ph Simon Upton; **46r** ph Jan Baldwin/Clare Mosley's house in London; **47al** ph Henry Bourne; **47bl** Simon Upton; **47br** ph Henry Bourne; **48l** ph Chris Everard/Suze Orman's apartment in New York designed by Patricia Seidman of Mullman Seidman Architects; **48–49** ph Jan Baldwin/Peter & Nicole Dawes' apartment, designed by Mullman Seidman Architects; **49br** ph Chris Everard/Peter and Nicole Dawes' apartment, designed by Mullman Seidman Architects; **50l** ph Chris Everard/an apartment in Paris, designed by architect Paul Collier;

50r ph Chris Everard/John Kifner's apartment in New York, designed by Mullman Seidman Architects; **51l** ph Andrew Wood/an apartment in Bath designed by Briffa Phillips Architects; **51r** ph Chris Everard/a London apartment designed by architect Gavin Jackson; **52al** ph Chris Everard/Programmable House in London, designed by d-squared; **52ar** ph Chris Everard/an apartment in Milan designed by Tito Canella of Canella & Achilli Architects; **52bl** ph Chris Everard/an apartment in Paris, designed by architect Paul Collier; **52–53** ph Chris Everard/an apartment in Paris designed by architects Guillaume Terver and Fabienne Couvert of cxt sarl d'architecture; **53r** ph Chris Everard/Pemper and Rabiner home in New York, designed by David Khouri of Comma; **54l** ph Chris Everard/Kampfner's house in London designed by Ash Sakula Architects; **54–55** ph Debi Treloar/an apartment in London by Malin Iovino Design; **55br** ph Debi Treloar/David & Macarena Wheldon's house in London designed by Fiona McLean; **56** ph Debi Treloar/Imogen Chappel's home in Suffolk; **57l** ph James Merrell; **57al** ph Chris Everard/a house in London designed by Helen Ellery of The Plot London; **57ar** ph Debi Treloar/Victoria Andreae's house in London; **57cl** ph Henry Bourne; **57cr** ph Andrew Wood/the London flat of Miles Johnson & Frank Ronan; **58al** ph Debi Treloar; **58c** ph Vanessa Davies; **58b** ph Henry Bourne; **58–59** ph Debi Treloar/Paul Balland and Jane Wadham of jwflowers.com's family home in London; **59bl** ph Debi Treloar/Sophie Eadie's house in London; **59br** ph Debi Treloar/Imogen Chappel's home in Suffolk.

Architects and Designers whose work is featured in this book

27.12 Design Ltd.
212 727 8169
www.2712design.com
Page 3

Ash Sakula Architects
+44 20 7837 9735
www.ashsak.com
Pages 9, 25a, 25cl, 54l

Azman Owens, Architects
+44 20 7354 2955
Page 23br

Felix Bonnier
+ 33 1 42 26 09 83
Pages 30bc, 32l, 39ar

Bowles & Linares
+44 20 7229 9886
Page 12l

Briffa Phillips
+44 1727 840567
Page 51l

Brookes Stacey Randall
+44 20 7403 0707
www.bsr-architects.com
Page 8r

Tito Canella
Canella & Achilli Architects
Milan
+39 024695222
www.canella-achilli.com
Page 52ar

Imogen Chappel
+44 7803 156081
Pages 56, 59br

Christopher Leach Design Ltd
+44 20 7235 2648
mail@christopherleach.com
Page 39l

Circus Architects
+44 20 7833 1999
Page 26l

Paul Collier, Architect
+ 33 1 53 72 49 32
paul.collier@architecte.net
Pages 50l, 52bl

Constanze von Unruh
Constanze Interior Projects
+44 20 8948 5533
constanze@constanzeinterior
projects.com
Pages 19br, 33l

Fabienne Couvert &
Guillaume Terver
cxt sarl d'architecture
+ 33 1 55 34 9850
www.couverterver-architectes.com
Pages 52–53

d-squared design
+44 20 7739 2632
dsquared@globalnet.co.uk
Page 52al

DAD Associates
+44 20 7336 6488
Page 24l

Dirand Joseph Architecture
tel/fax. +33 01 47 97 78 57
JOSEPH.dirand@wanadoo.fr
Front cover

Helen Ellery
The Plot London
+44 20 7251 8116
www.theplotlondon.com
Pages 22l, 43ar, 57al

Nicole Fabre
592 King's Rd
London SW6 2DX, UK
+44 20 7384 3112
Page 44

Alex Fairweather
Clothes and Textiles
Mobile. +44 7929 359425
Page 43

Filer & Cox
+44 20 7357 7574
www.filerandcox.com
Pages 20a, 32–33

Gabellini Associates
212 388 1700
Page 19l

Gavin Jackson Architects
+44 7050 097561
Pages 41l, 51r

Grace & Favour
35 North Cross Rd
East Dulwich
London SE22 9ET, UK
Page 43

Lulu Guinness
+44 20 7823 4828
www.luluguinness.com
Page 1

Yves Halard, Interior Decoration
+ 33 1 44 07 14 00
Page 15l

Alastair Hendy
Food writer, art director
and designer
fax: +44 20 7739 6040
Pages 15r, 20bl, 25bc

Guy Hills
Photographer
+44 20 7916 2610
guyhills@hotmail.com
Page 33r

Hirst Pacific Ltd
212 625 3670
hirstpacific@earthlink.net
Page 38r

jwflowers.com
+44 20 7735 7771
www.jwflowers.com
Pages 58–59

John Barman Inc.
212 838 9443
www.johnbarman.com
Page 28l

Clark Johnson, Lighting
Consultant
Johnson Schwinghammer
212 643 1552
Page 53r

Jonathan Clark Architects
+44 20 7286 5676
jonathan@jonathanclark
    architects.co.uk
Page 39br

David Khouri
Comma
212 420 7866
www.comma-nyc.com
Page 53r

Kim Sully Antiques
+44 1483 579652
Mobile. 07710 769230
Page 44

Bruno & Hélène Lafforgue
Mas de l'Ange
Maison d'Hôte
Petite route de
St. Remy-de-Provence
13946 Mollégès, France
Page 47bl

Laura Bohn Design
Associates, Inc.
212 645 3636
Page 14ar

Fiona McLean
McLean Quinlan Architects
+44 20 8767 1633
Page 55br

Maisonette
+44 20 8964 8444
maisonetteUK@aol.com
Page 30a

Malin Iovino Design
tel/fax. +44 20 7252 3542
lovino@btinternet.com
Page 54–55

Mark Brook Design
+44 20 7221 8106
Page 26c

Mark Guard Architects
+44 20 7380 1199
Page 24r

The Moderns
212 387 8852
moderns@aol.com
Page 39cr

Moneo Brock Studio
212 625 0308
www.moneobrock.com
Pages 10b, 14al, 16a

Clare Mosley
Gilding, églomisé panels,
lamps
+44 20 7708 3123
Page 46r

Mullman Seidman Architects
212 431 0770
www.mullmanseidman.com
Pages 11r, 12r, 14bl, 48l,
48–49, 49br, 50r

François Muracciole, Architect
+ 33 1 43 71 33 03
francois.muracciole@libertysurf.fr
Page 30br

Michael Nathenson
Unique Environments
+44 20 7431 6978
www.unique-environments.co.uk
Page 19ar

Nico Rensch Architeam
+44 7711 412898
Pages 11l, 28r

Ou Baholyodhin Studio
+44 20 7426 0666
www.ou-b.com
Page 40br

Retrouvius Reclamation & Design
tel/fax. +44 20 7724 3387
Page 33r

Luigi Rosselli
+ 61 2 9281 1498
Pages 8l, 23bcl

Lucy Salem
+44 20 8563 2625
lucyandmarcsalem@hotmail.com
Page 43bl

Schack-Arnott
Danish Classic Moderne
+ 61 3 9525 0250
Page 29br

Steven Sclaroff, Designer
212 691 7814
sclaroff@aol.com
Page 32r

Sheppard Day Design
+44 20 7821 2002
Page 13

Site Specific Ltd
+44 20 7490 3176
www.sitespecificltd.co.uk
Page 38l

Seth Stein, Architect
+44 20 8968 8581
admin@sethstein.com
Pages 26r, 41br

Steven Learner Studio
212 741 8583
www.stevenlearnerstudio.com
Page 21

Touch Interior Design
+44 20 7498 6409
Page 14br

Urban Salon Ltd
+44 20 7357 8800
Pages 34–35

VX design & architecture
tel/fax. +44 20 7370 5496
www.vxdesign.com
Pages 23bcr, 41ar

Voon Wong Architects
+44 20 7587 0116
voon@dircon.co.uk
Pages 22r, 40a

Woodhams Landscape Ltd
+44 20 7346 5656
www.woodhams.co.uk
Showroom:
+44 20 7300 0777
Pages 17br, 26c

Yves-Claude Design
www.kanso.com
Pages 12c, 16br, 36–37

Consuelo Zoelly
+ 33 42 62 19 95
Page 20br

index

Figures in *italics* refer to captions.

A

appliances 11, 51–52
cooktops *28*, 32–33
freezers *28*, 31
fridges *28*, 31
ovens 32–33

B

backsplashes 19–21, *19, 20*
blackboards 54, *55*, 58
breakfast bar *11*
built-in kitchens *11*, 14–15
built-in or not? 14–15

C

cabinets
built-in 14–15, 38
freestanding 14–15, *17*
sheer-fronted *14*, 38
stainless steel *37*, 38–39
wood 39, *43*
ceramic 57
sinks *22*, 29, *43, 45*
chairs *39, 55*, 58
chopping boards *16, 19*, 19
color 38, 54, 57, *57*, 58
compact kitchens 48–53
composites 20, *20, 23*
concrete 20, 21, 24, 38
contemporary kitchens 36–41
cooktops 32–33
Corian 20, 21, 38
cork 23, 24
corner space *17*, 51

countertops 18–21
concrete 20–21, 38
Corian 20–21, 38
laminate 20, *20*, 21
stainless steel 19–21, 38–39
stone 20–21, 38
wood *19*, 19, 21
country kitchens 42–47
cupboards and cabinets
built-in 14, 38, 44, 49
fridge 31
handles 14
lighting 27
planning 8–11

D

details and ergonomics 16–17
dining areas *8, 11, 55*
dishwashers 51
display *14, 44*
draining board 29–30

E

electrical sockets 26–27, 39
electrics 10–11, 26–27
extensions 8
extractor hoods 49

F

fabrics *43, 44*
family-friendly kitchens 54–59
faucets
sinks and 29–30
with flexible spouts *30*
fixtures 28–33
flooring 22–24, 44
brick 23

concrete 24
finishes 23
linoleum 23–24
metal 23, *24*
rubber 23, *23*
stone 22–24
tiles *22, 23*
vinyl 23–24
wood 22–24, *22, 24, 43, 44*
freestanding kitchens 14–15
freezers 10, 31
fridge-freezers *9*, 31, *55*
fridges 10, 31
furniture 45, 56

G

galley kitchens 48
gas supply 11, 33

H

handles 14
hanging rack *8–9, 14, 51*
home office 8
hutches 14, 51

IJ

island units *9*
Jacobsen, Arne *39*

L

laminate 20, 21
laundry 8
layout 11, 50
lighting 10, 11, 25–27, 51, *51, 53, 57, 59*
linoleum 22, 57

M

marble 20, 23, *37*
microwave ovens *32*
modern kitchens 36–41, 50

O

open-plan kitchens *8*, 54, *55*
ovens 32–33

P

pantry 14
parquet flooring *22*
planning the space 8–11
play areas 56, 58
plinths 51–52
plumbing 10–11
pot stands *16*

R

ranges 32–33, 42, 44
refrigerator *see* fridge
retro *45*
room divider *8*
rubber 23, *23*

S

safety 56–57, 59
salvage 44
Scandinavian-look 45
Shaker style 45, *45*
shelving
glass-fronted *12*
open *12*, 14, *50*
sinks
and faucets 29–30
ceramic *22*, 29, *43, 45*
double 29
stainless steel *28*
wooden "chest" *29*

slate *16*, 18–23
stainless steel
cart *14, 17*
counters *19*, 19–21, 38
flooring 23
fridge *28*
sink *28*
splashbacks 19–20, *19*
units *37*, 38–39
steps 58
stone
finishes 20, 23, 57
flooring 22, 24
work surfaces 20, 21, 38
storage 12–17
stoves 32–33, 42, 44
surfaces 18–21

T

tables *38*, 42, 57
tiling
backsplash *20*
flooring *22, 23*
Sterlingboard *23*

V

vinyl 23–24, 57

W

washing machine 51, 53
water softener 30
wood
cabinets 39, *43*
counters *18–19*, 19, 21
finishes 19, 23, 57, *57*
flooring 22, *22, 24, 43, 44*